PRESENTED TO

_____

BY

_____

To my son Alan,
a fine young man who loves life—
and loves this game!

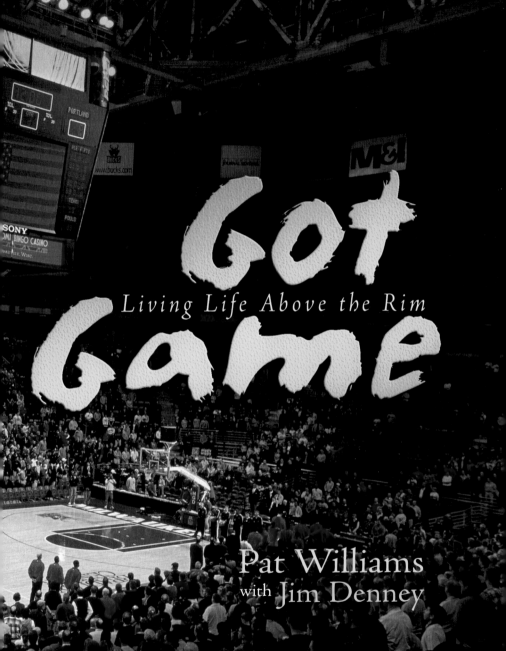

Got

Living Life Above the Rim

Game

Pat Williams
with Jim Denney

J. Countryman
Nashville, Tennessee

Contents

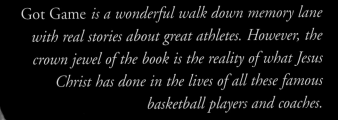

In a world that seems to focus on the negative surrounding the professional athlete, it is very refreshing to get a glimpse of some real champions. These athletes understand that basketball is a means to an end, and what lasts forever is a relationship with our heavenly Father, which comes from knowing Jesus Christ. These are extraordinary athletes who have not forgotten the giver of their gifts and have allowed God to propel them to play and live at a higher standard.

BRENT PRICE
NBA PLAYER

Got Game *addresses the most important aspect of life—our relationship to God. Through the lives of NBA players and coaches, Pat Williams shares how God can become relevant in your life too.*

BOBBY JONES
FORMER NBA PLAYER

Got Game *is a wonderful walk down memory lane with real stories about great athletes. However, the crown jewel of the book is the reality of what Jesus Christ has done in the lives of all these famous basketball players and coaches.*

JON MCGLOCKLIN
FORMER NBA PLAYER

Pat Williams has blended basketball and spirituality and the end result will thrill your heart and make a difference in your life.

BRYCE DREW
NBA PLAYER

From the driveway
    to the playground
to the downtown arena,
    this is the game.
Whether played on concrete,
    asphalt, or hardwood,
this is America's game.

How 'bout you?
Did you bring your game?

Show me your no-look pass,
your crossover dribble,
your Ankle-Breaking Moves,
your high-flying rejections.

got SkiLLs?
GOT JUMP?

Show me what you got.

Oh, yeah. Nice move.

YOU GOT GAME.

by *David Robinson*
CENTER, #50,
SAN ANTONIO SPURS

Foreword

FOREWORD

The game of basketball teaches us a lot about life.

Nobody wins games by just stepping out on the court and hoping to be the best. It takes a great deal of preparation. It's nice to know that you've prepared your body, you've studied your opponent, and you are sufficiently motivated to do your best. It is difficult, if not impossible, to succeed without this preparation.

Sometimes, in life, people try to get by without the proper preparation. It's not going to work! We need to understand that there is a lot more to this life than just going out and hoping for the best. We can prepare ourselves for the ups and downs of life and be a winner with the proper focus on Jesus Christ.

Nobody likes a player who is selfish and out for himself. Every team has had a player who only cares about his statistics and his contract. Teams want players who can sacrifice for the success of the team. Pat Williams has spent his life in pro basketball as a former general manager of the Philadelphia 76ers, the Chicago Bulls, the Atlanta Hawks, and now as senior vice president of the team he helped build from the ground up, the Orlando Magic. He also has a deep understanding of spiritual truth and an abiding commitment to Jesus Christ.

The book you hold in your hands is full of wisdom, excitement, and power. It includes the profound and practical life lessons that come from the words of great NBA players, from dramatic stories, and even from off-the-wall anecdotes. Pat Williams is one of the greatest motivators I know, and these stories will inspire you to live your life "above the rim."

So turn the page and enter the arena. Pat has saved you a seat at center court.

David M. Robinson

This game is not just about winning. It's about joy!

I Love This Game

CHAPTER 1

Want to know what an NBA championship ring looks like? Here, I'll show you mine. See that inscription? It reads, "Defense and Persevere." No, I never wear the ring. That would be like wearing an electric toaster on your knuckle! But every once in a while I take it out of the box and look at it—

And I remember that championship season.

I got my start in the NBA in 1968, when Jack Ramsay of the Philadelphia 76ers hired me as business manager. I was general manager of the Chicago Bulls for four years, then bounced over to the Atlanta Hawks for a year, then rebounded to the 76ers, where I served as general manager for twelve seasons.

We assembled an incredible team in my first years in Philly. We had Bobby Jones, an ambidextrous shooter and great passer with a quiet, self-effacing demeanor. Bobby was nicknamed "the White Shadow" for his tall, gaunt physique.

Bobby paired up at forward with Julius Winfield Erving II—the legendary Dr. J— whom we acquired from the New York Nets in 1976. Doc was the Michael Jordan of the 1970s and early '80s, the most recognized athlete of his time. They called him "Doctor" because of the dignified, professional way he "operated" on the court. At 6' 6", Dr. J was long and lean, with telescopic arms and big hands like baseball gloves. He was "the Doctor of Dunk," able to repeal the laws of gravity and leap tall buildings with a single bound. He played basketball jazz, setting a syncopated tempo on the court, finding a rhythm and improvising all the way. His demeanor was businesslike and professional—pure focus, no theatrics,

no trash-talk. He had a tireless work ethic, a contagious optimism, and he never gave less than 1,000 percent. (Julius remains a close friend of mine to this day; I have the privilege of working alongside him in the Orlando Magic organization.)

At point guard, we had an amazing athlete: Maurice Cheeks, a soft-spoken, gum-chewing ball-distributor, and an unselfish leader in assists, with a keen grasp of both the fundamentals and the subtleties of the game. Mo's quick hands made him an uncannily effective ball-stealer. (He would eventually set a record of 2,310 career steals—an NBA theft record that stood until John Stockton broke it in 1996). Mo Cheeks was a team-player who worked well within coach Billy Cunningham's carefully designed game plan.

Our shooting guard was Andrew Toney, who became a two-time NBA All-Star with the 76ers. A confident, consistent scorer (he averaged 15.9

points and 4.2 assists over an eight-year career), Andrew was famous for his hot streaks. When Toney had the hot hand, he was unstoppable.

At center we had the immortal Moses Malone, who would ultimately enjoy a twenty-one-year pro career and a spot on the NBA's All-Time Top 50 Team. In 1983, as the Sixers made their championship run, Moses was on his way to his third league MVP award. He was a tireless athlete, a consistent scorer, and one of the greatest offensive rebounders to ever play the game. I once calculated that we were paying him around $500 a minute—and it was a bargain. He had an unusual tendency to talk about himself in the third person: "It's never easy for Moses. Moses got to get out every night and work hard."

"Everybody in this league has to realize why they started playing. It wasn't for money, it wasn't for the attention and the crowd. It was for the joy. You got skills, I got skills, let's get started. When someone sees me play, I want them to think, 'Man, that guy loves this game!' . . . It's about fun and joy."

KEVIN GARNETT
FORWARD,
MINNESOTA TIMBERWOLVES

"Fo' . . . Fo' . . . Fo'!"

For the 1982-83 season, the 76ers owner, Harold Katz, demanded a new style of play from the 76ers: *physical.* "This is a team of nice guys," he said. "We lead the NBA in helping guys to their feet. That's gotta stop. I want this team to lead the NBA in knocking guys on

their can." Well,
Moses Malone
was the man for
the job. He thrived
on physical contact—
the rougher it got, the better
he played.

In that season, the Sixers amassed a record
of 65 wins, 17 losses—best in the league.
We broke all previous club attendance records
and clinched the first round playoff bye.
Then, just days before the playoffs,
disaster struck: Moses Malone came
down with tendonitis in both knees.
Suddenly, our indestructible man
in the pivot couldn't even walk.
I'll never forget the sick feeling
in my stomach as I saw Moses
lifted out of a car and carried
into the hospital for X rays.

Incredibly upbeat, Moses predicted
he would play and the Sixers
would sweep the playoffs. The way
he put it was "Fo' . . . Fo' . . . Fo'!"

In other words, four wins, no losses, a clean sweep. No team in playoffs history had ever done better than 12 and 2—and Moses was predicting 12 and 0. He sensed a destiny for our team and was determined to see it through, regardless of his throbbing knees.

The Sixers faced the New York Knicks in the quarterfinals, beginning with a home game at the Spectrum. Moses spent most of his free time with bags of ice strapped to his knees. On the floor, he scored 38 points, 17 rebounds, and no limps. We captured Game 1, 112-102. We played Game 2 minus Bobby Jones (flu) and Andrew Toney (deep thigh bruise), and fell behind by 20. Late in the game, we stunned the Knicks with a 22 to 1 run, winning it 98-91. Game 3 at Madison Square Garden was a heart-stopper all the way. It was tied at 105 with four seconds remaining when Franklin Edwards (subbing for Toney) hit a sweet ten-foot jumper to win it, 107-105. Game 4 was appropriately played on May 1, because it was "Mayday!" for the Knicks. Julius Erving and Moses Malone shone down the stretch to collect the win. The first third of Moses' "Fo' . . . Fo' . . . Fo'!" prediction had come true. Despite his pain, Moses had scored 125 points and grabbed 62 rebounds in the series.

Our semifinals opponent was the Milwaukee Bucks. Game 1 on May 8 was at home—an epic battle that could not be contained within a mere 48 minutes. The Bucks and Sixers grappled mightily into overtime. With 96 seconds left in OT, the Bucks led by one. Then Bobby Jones intercepted an inbounds pass and fed it to Clint Richardson at the hole, who jammed it home for the lead. That basket, plus a foul shot, sealed a Sixers win, 111 to 109. Game 2 was a tough defensive battle at both ends, as demonstrated by the low score: Sixers 87, Bucks 81. In Game 3, at Milwaukee Arena, the Sixers fell behind by 7, then battled back in the fourth quarter with a 33-point run. Philly won, 104 to 96. In Game 4, the Sixers came up short: Milwaukee 100, Philadelphia 94. Moses Malone was philosophical when his prediction was overturned. "Okay," he said, grinning, "make it fo'-*five*-fo'." For Game 5, the Sixers came loaded with buckshot. Andrew Toney collected 30 points, Moses 28, and Doc 24. Final score: Sixers 115, Bucks 103.

Worth the Wait

"In the NBA, you have to take fun seriously."
BOB HILL
FORMER COACH,
NEW YORK KNICKS,
INDIANA PACERS, AND
SAN ANTONIO SPURS

Now it was on to the finals—the Philadelphia 76ers versus the defending champions, the L.A. Lakers. These were the Lakers of legend: Kareem Abdul-Jabbar, Magic Johnson, Bob McAdoo, Jamaal "Silk" Wilkes, and Norm Nixon. They had conquered the San Antonio Spurs in six. On Sunday, May 22, the Lakers rumbled into the Spectrum.

Game 1 was a close contest through four quarters. With less than two minutes left, the Sixers were up by 8—then everything seemed to go wrong. In their next four possessions, the Sixers turned the ball over three times and missed two free throws. The game was saved by a flurry of rebounds by Doc, Bobby, and Moses. It was ugly, but it was a win—113 to 107. Game 2 turned on fouls (Sixers 16, Lakers 29) and free throws (Sixers 23, Lakers 3). The Sixers won it, 103 to 93. In Game 3, at the Forum in L.A., the Lakers surged to a 15-point lead in the second quarter. But the Sixers never panicked. By the end of the third quarter, we had battled back to a 72-72 tie—and the momentum was

on our side. A 14-zero Sixers run in the fourth quarter left Magic Johnson and the Lakers in disarray. We won, 111 to 94. For the third time in a row, the Sixers had overcome a Lakers halftime lead to win. Afterwards, coach Billy Cunningham announced, "We want L.A. in four. We want people to remember this team."

Game 4 was on Tuesday, May 31. As was our wont, we fell behind early, trailing by 16, but battled back to a one-point lead late in the fourth. In the defining moment of the game, Doc had the ball at the top of the key with six seconds left on the shot clock. There was no one open, and no time to drive. So he jumped and pulled the trigger. From eighteen feet away, the ball unerringly found the hole. At that instant, Julius Erving earned his ring. No, the game wasn't over, but the Lakers were psychologically defeated by that shot. The final score was Sixers 115, Lakers 108. We were the NBA champions, and we had done it with a playoff record that has never been topped—12 wins, 1 loss. (The Lakers achieved a record of 15 and 1 in the 2001 playoffs; there is, of course, one more playoff round today than in those days).

After the game, I hurried to the locker room to join the celebration. It was an absolute mob scene. I've never seen such joy and elation as I saw that night. Dr. J, who had worked to bring a championship to Philly since 1976, raised the trophy high. "Seven years is a long time," he said, grinning broadly, "but it was worth the wait!"

The Joy of the Game

Returning to Philly, the Sixers were accorded a victory parade, complete with confetti, from Center City to Veterans Stadium. An estimated one million fans lined the parade route, and another fifty-five thousand fans filled the Vet. As the stadium rocked with applause, Doc lifted the championship trophy in one hand and embraced Coach Cunningham with the other.

I was on the podium behind Doc and Billy, and the sight, sounds, and emotions of that moment are etched in my memory. It was not only a portrait of victory—it was a picture of absolute elation and consummate joy. That is why the game is played. That is why it is so exciting. That is why one of the most fitting slogans of the NBA is "I Love This Game!"

"Play skillfully with a shout of joy."

PSALM 33:3

Is there a more fast-paced, adrenaline-pumping, stomach-twisting, heart-shuddering game on the planet? No way! I can't count the times I've stood courtside, biting my fingernails to the elbow as one of my teams battled mightily for the win—and I've loved every Maalox moment of it!

Sure, I can recall times of crushing, painful defeat. But if you ask me what I think of when I hear the word "basketball," all that comes to mind are images of *joy*. I think of Magic Johnson playing the game with a smile so wide it has to be continued on the next face! I think of Michael Jordan sailing through the air, feet pumping as if he is racing up invisible stairs, tongue hanging, eyes alight with childlike delight, as if even *he* is amazed that he can do such an impossible thing! I think of the boyish grin, bright as a searchlight, radiating from the face of Shaquille O'Neal after a big win.

All the multimillion-dollar deals, the agents, the hype, the limousines, the product endorsements, the fans—that's not what these guys play for. It's not about the money or the fame or the stats or a place in the history books. They play for the *love* of the game. They play for the *joy* of the game.

Basketball is the ultimate playground game—a color-splashed, lightning-fast, soaring, dunking, showtime game. It's a game of thrills, a game of joy—and there is nothing else like it in the world.

1953—The Cooz in Four OTs:

Some called him "The Houdini of the Hardwood" because of his dazzling ball-handling and playmaking talents. Others just called him "The Cooz." Though he played in a slower-paced era (there was no 24-second clock to force a team to shoot), Bob Cousy could have excelled easily in today's fast-break, high-pressure game.

The Era of Cousy and Baylor

In the 1953 NBA playoffs, Cousy and the Boston Celtics faced the Syracuse Nationals. Boston's legendary coach, Red Auerbach, created a strategy around Bob Cousy: get the ball to Cooz and let him dribble until he's fouled. It worked. In regulation play plus four overtimes, Cousy scored 20 points from the floor, attempted 32 free throws (of which he made 30), and walked away with a then-record 50 points. In a test of sheer endurance, Boston won, 111 to 105.

1958—Payback for Big Blue:

The era of the 1950s was dominated by the fierce rivalry between the Boston Celtics and the St. Louis Hawks. The first of their four title clashes was in the 1957 NBA Finals, in which the Celtics barely prevailed. (It was the first of Boston's record sixteen championships). Game 7 was decided by a 125 to 123 Boston victory in double-OT. That game came within an eyelash of going to a third overtime as Hawks forward Bob Pettit attempted a shot at the buzzer. The ball made one heart-stopping circuit of the rim—then fell outside of the hoop. But Big Blue's day would come. (Pettit was nicknamed "Big Blue" by announcer Buddy Blattner because of the long blue coat Pettit wore on the street.)

The same teams met the following year in the '58 Finals. Going into Game 6 of that series in St. Louis, the Hawks were up three games to two. Playing for payback after the previous year's loss, Big Blue had a career night. Pettit scored 31 points in the first three quarters of Game 6. Then he unleashed even more firepower, accounting for 19 of his team's 21 fourth-quarter points. He tipped in his last two points with 15 seconds remaining, putting the Hawks up by three. The Celtics scored one more basket before the final buzzer, cutting the Hawks victory margin to a single point.

That 110 to 109 win gave Big Blue his payback—and gave the Hawks their one and only NBA title. Pettit's 50 points matched the playoff record set by Bob Cousy in 1953. (The current playoff record is 63 points set by Elgin Baylor in 1962, tied by Michael Jordan in 1986 in double OT).

1960—Baylor's 71: The Lakers, newly relocated from Minnesota to Los Angeles, were led by a fabulous shooter, Elgin Baylor. His average for the 1960-61 season was 34.8 points a game (second only to Wilt Chamberlain's 38.4). On November 15, 1960, Baylor went to New York and singlehandedly scored 71 points against the

Knicks, a then-record high for most points in a game. (His 25 rebounds for the night? A mere footnote.)

After the game, Baylor shared a cab with roommate "Hot Rod" Hundley (now an announcer for the Utah Jazz). Hot Rod had scored 2 points in the game. Said Hundley as the cab took them to their hotel, "Man, what a night we had! Seventy-three points between us!"

The harder you work,
the luckier you get.

Work the Ball

If you're an NBA player less than six feet tall, count on it: They're gonna call you "Shorty." Unless, that is, your name is Avery Johnson.

A. J. may be a 5' 11" point guard, but he has earned the respect of his taller colleagues on the court. He has also earned a championship ring—but not before proving himself worthy.

In 1988, he was passed over in the NBA draft because the scouts didn't think he was big enough. But Johnson didn't let that stop him. He spent a year with the Palm Beach Stingrays of the U.S. Basketball League, then landed a spot with the Seattle SuperSonics, spending two seasons on the bench. Next stop: the Denver Nuggets—where he was waived on Christmas Eve, less than three months after his arrival. He was picked up by the San Antonio Spurs and waived again the following Christmas. Johnson spent the 1991-92 season on the Houston Rockets' bench, then bounced back to the Spurs the following season.

"When those things happen," A. J. recalls, "the human part of you gets discouraged. But then your faith kicks in and says to keep on going." Johnson's faith paid off. He got his chance in the 1993-94 season, when he was a backup to Tim Hardaway of the Golden State Warriors. Hardaway blew out a knee in the preseason, which made A. J. the starting point guard. Johnson went out and averaged 10.9 points and 5.3 assists per game. But when Hardaway returned, the Warriors gave A. J. his walking papers.

Through it all, Avery Johnson maintained his focus, optimism, and determination. He continued his workouts and weight training. He spent hundreds of hours practicing his shot. It worked. Over his first seven years in the NBA, his shooting percentage steadily rose from 34.9 to 51.9. The Spurs took notice, and in 1994 the team signed him for the third and final time. He remained with the Spurs for seven years until he signed with the Denver Nuggets in the summer of 2001.

Spurs head coach Gregg Popovich always considered A. J. the heart of the team. To put it bluntly, says Popovich, "No Avery, no team. He's got a heart bigger than the Alamodome. His work ethic is scary, and he's personable enough to be a leader. . . . He's not only a tremendous person, he's a much better basketball player than anybody has ever given him credit for."

A. J. and Ai

Avery Johnson has proven himself with his prudent shot selection, confident ball-handling, and unselfish attitude—but he has particularly excelled as a defender. It was the defensive prowess of Johnson and the Spurs that brought San Antonio its first NBA title. Adopting a strategy they called "grinding it out," the Spurs chose to wear teams down instead of blowing them out. As center David Robinson put it, "Teams know that for 48 minutes, we're not going anywhere."

Avery Johnson described his role in the Spurs' formidable transition defense: "The main thing I want to do," he said, "is slow the other team down a bit so that my teammates can get back to help. Often, though, I have to try to stop the ball myself. As soon as we miss a shot, I'll sprint back to the top of the key at the other end so I can get a clear view of the break and see who's coming. Once I've done that, I try to pick out the main threat. Is it the shooter on the wing or the point guard coming at me at 150 miles an hour? What are each guy's strengths and weaknesses? Is the point guard better at pulling up and shooting the three, à la Tim Hardaway or Stephon Marbury, or is he better at getting to the basket, like Jason Kidd or John Stockton? . . . These are things I have to think about, and I only have a split second."

A. J.'s intensity on the court is closely linked to his intense faith in God. When he speaks, he freely blends basketball metaphor with Scripture. Before the last regular season game of the Spurs' 1998-99 championship run, Johnson gave his teammates a fiery sermon from Joshua chapter 7. He wanted to make sure that his team, having just plowed through their toughest opponents, Utah and Portland, did not succumb to overconfidence against the Golden State Warriors. Only by beating the Warriors in the last game of the season could the Spurs secure the home court advantage throughout the playoffs.

So Johnson told his teammates the story of Joshua and the army of the Israelites, who swiftly defeated Jericho by God's hand. Swelled with pride after their victory, the Israelites planned to attack the little podunk village of Ai. What the Israelites didn't know was that one of their teammates, Achan, had let down his spiritual guard, secretly sinning against God's commands. What's more, the overconfident Israelites only committed a small force of "second-stringers" to attack Ai. The result, according to Preacher Johnson: "They got busted in the mouth!"

The moral of the story: No player can afford to let down, not even a little. Every opponent must be approached as if it were Jericho itself.

After Johnson's sermon, his teammates whipped the Warriors, 88 to 81, securing the home court advantage in the playoffs. In the postseason, they went on to beat the Minnesota Timberwolves, the L.A. Lakers, the Portland Trailblazers, and the New York Knicks to win the 1999 NBA title.

The Bravery of Avery

Another biblical story that comes to mind when you watch Johnson play is the story of David and Goliath. It takes an extra measure of skill, quickness, and survival instinct for a 5' 11" guard to hold his own among a bunch of Philistines who are a head taller and one hundred pounds heavier than he is. A. J. doesn't hesitate to draw a charge—even when it's like squaring up against a speeding locomotive.

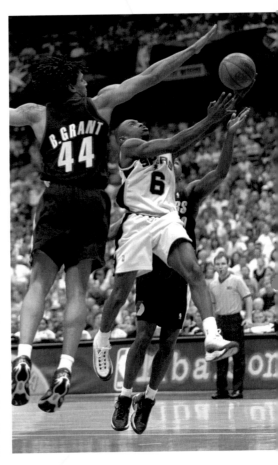

On one occasion, in a home game against the Lakers, A. J. set himself against an onrushing Shaquille O'Neal—and *kazaam*!

Johnson found himself sprawled on the paint. "I hit the floor real hard," he recalled after his head cleared. "Shaq landed right next to me. If he'd fallen on top of me, I don't know if we'd be talking right now." The next day at practice, Avery's teammates marked the "crime scene," placing white tape on the floor in the shape of his body. "If you're going to try to stop a big guy," A. J. concludes, "just make sure it's worth it."

Players like A. J. and center David Robinson helped set an emotional, moral, and spiritual tone for the San Antonio Spurs. As a result, the Spurs developed a reputation for exemplary behavior. The *Sporting News* called the Spurs "the antithesis of all that is wrong with today's pro hoopsters. The Spurs don't talk trash, swagger, leave their jerseys untucked, pierce their bodies . . . or curse at reporters."

"Bring Your Game, Not Your Name!"

With the vastly underrated abilities of 5' 11" Avery Johnson, the scoring power of soft-spoken 7' forward Tim Duncan, and the rebounding and shot-blocking of 7' 1" center David Robinson, the Spurs defeated the New York Knicks in 1999, bringing home the team's first world championship in its twenty-six-year

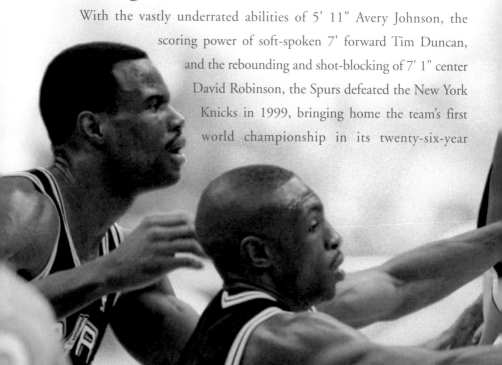

existence. From the Alamodome to Madison Square Garden, it was one of the most exciting finals series in NBA history.

Game 1, June 16, 1999, San Antonio. Despite predictions that the twenty-three-year-old Duncan would choke in his first NBA finals game, the Spurs forward stayed loose, collecting 33 points and 16 rebounds. Duncan and Robinson kept the Knicks busy inside, opening up opportunities for outside shooter Jaren Jackson, who nailed 5 of 10 treys. The Spurs' defense wore the Knicks offense to a nub. In the fourth quarter, Knicks' offensive leaders Latrell Sprewell and Allan Houston combined for a mere 1 of 12, thanks to Robinson's presence at the hole. Final score: San Antonio 89, New York 77.

Game 2, June 18, 1999, San Antonio. The Spurs held the Knicks' shooting to 33 percent from the field and 2 of 14

from three-point range. Coach Popovich was exultant, calling the game "our best defensive effort of the season." Duncan and Robinson blocked nine shots between them. Final score: San Antonio 80, New York 67. The game ended with the Alamodome rocking to chants of "Sweep! Sweep!" But Avery Johnson exhorted his brethren, "Focus, focus! Bring your game, not your name!"

Game 3, June 21, 1999, New York. The Spurs had dominated the first two games, but in Game 3, the Knicks controlled the tempo and knocked

San Antonio's offense out of sync. New York's Allan Houston turned in a career performance (34 points); Sprewell ignited down the stretch (24 points, including 10 in the fourth quarter); and forward Larry Johnson added 16 points to the Knicks total. New York had the superior defense that night, forcing 20 turnovers and holding Tim Duncan scoreless from the field in the final quarter. Avery Johnson mused, "We've got a series on our hands." Final score: New York 89, San Antonio 81.

Game 4, June 23, 1999, New York. The big question after Game 3: How will the Spurs handle the loss? David Robinson's answer proved prophetic: "This team has always bounced back well after a loss. Always. I think it gives us a healthy anger." The Spurs went right back to grinding it out. Duncan and Robinson dominated the boards. All five Spurs starters—Duncan, Robinson, Johnson, Sean Elliott, and Mario Elie—scored in double digits. Whenever the Knicks were about to rally, Elie would snuff their morale with a trey. Avery Johnson—more famous for assists than shooting—stunned the Knicks with penetration and layups, scoring 14 points. Final score: San Antonio 96, New York 89.

Game 5, June 25, 1999, New York. Though the Knicks were on the ropes, the Spurs avoided overconfidence. "We're still in a fight," said Avery, "and we have to stay focused." Wise words, because the Knicks' Latrell Sprewell put on a show that night, scoring 35 points, including 14 in the fourth quarter. The Spurs stayed close while wearing the Knicks down.

"But let each one examine his own work, and then he will have rejoicing in himself alone, and not in another."

GALATIANS 6:4

When Avery Johnson put the Spurs on top by one with an eighteen-foot jumper, there were 47 seconds left to play. Sprewell answered with a fifteen-foot shot—but missed. He got another desperate chance with 2.1 seconds left. He took a pass under the basket from Charlie Ward, but Elliott and Duncan pinned him down at the baseline. Spree dribbled out, turned to launch the jumper—but found himself smothered by Robinson. The final buzzer sounded as the ball left Sprewell's fingers, falling way short.

The gold ring Avery Johnson wears is a glittering testimony to the power of hard work, focus, and dedication to a goal. It proves that you can't measure a man's greatness in feet and inches. Greatness can only be measured by the size of a man's heart. "I'm a guy that the normal American kid can look at," says A. J. "I'm five-eleven, I wear size ten shoes, and I'm the shortest guy on the court. . . . When I set goals in my life, they're not easy to attain. That's why I set them high, so I can really push myself. . . .

"My life has been pretty much a mountain, and I'm going straight up the mountain. It hasn't been a roller coaster; it's just been a mountain. It's been a pretty hard climb at parts of the mountain, but it just keeps getting better and better, and I know it's because God is walking with me."

Bucking the Odds

Charles Linwood "Buck" Williams started life as the son of North Carolina sharecroppers. By the end of his seventeen-year NBA career,

he had logged over 1,300 games, 16,000 points, and 13,000 rebounds. He was a three-time All-Star and played in two NBA Finals. In his long career, only one goal eluded him: an NBA championship. "I've come to the realization," he reflected, "that for some people a championship is not in the cards. I think that's really the only thing missing from my resumé."

Buck Williams attributes his longevity in the sport to the lessons he learned as a youngster—particularly lessons about hard work. "I've worked since I was twelve years old," he recalls, "in a warehouse stacking boxes, doing inventory, making deliveries, taking my turn at the cash registers. I learned that success is built on the American way: hard work. People can see when you work hard and they appreciate that. My father always said, 'Your good name means more than a million dollars in gold.'. . .

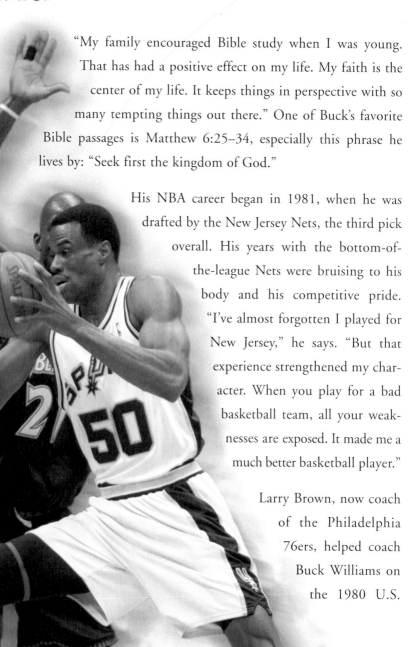

"My family encouraged Bible study when I was young. That has had a positive effect on my life. My faith is the center of my life. It keeps things in perspective with so many tempting things out there." One of Buck's favorite Bible passages is Matthew 6:25–34, especially this phrase he lives by: "Seek first the kingdom of God."

His NBA career began in 1981, when he was drafted by the New Jersey Nets, the third pick overall. His years with the bottom-of-the-league Nets were bruising to his body and his competitive pride. "I've almost forgotten I played for New Jersey," he says. "But that experience strengthened my character. When you play for a bad basketball team, all your weaknesses are exposed. It made me a much better basketball player."

Larry Brown, now coach of the Philadelphia 76ers, helped coach Buck Williams on the 1980 U.S.

Olympic team and was the head coach during Buck's first two years with the Nets. "I used to call him my son," Brown recalls. "He's what this league should be about: a guy who came to practice every day, who came to every game, who never took a minute off."

In 1989, Williams was traded to the Portland Trailblazers. Throughout his seven seasons there, the team never missed the playoffs and twice went to the finals. In 1996, he signed with the Knicks as a free agent and retired in 1999. Buck Williams has "bucked the odds" through seventeen years in the NBA. Some would say he was "lucky" to have had such a long career. But how does Buck Williams see it?

"There's an old locker room saying," he says. "'The harder you work, the luckier you get.' I try to use that motto in my life. It helps me keep my career on a solid note. I always set high goals because it makes me work hard. I always tell young people that it's not the most talented people who attain the most. It's the ones who work the hardest to achieve their goals."

Guys like Avery Johnson and Buck Williams believe in hard work— and they believe in God. They're living proof that those who succeed, whether in basketball or in life, are those who work hard and make their own luck.

The Era of Bill Russell and Wilt the Stilt

1962—Wilt's 100: Wilt Chamberlain dominated pro basketball from 1959 through 1973, playing for the Philadelphia (later San Francisco) Warriors, the Philadelphia 76ers, and the Los Angeles Lakers. He scored 31,419 points, averaging 30.1 points for his career. On March 2, 1962, he astonished the world by scoring 100 points in a single game, the Warriors' 169-147 drubbing of the New York Knicks in Hershey, Pennsylvania.

1962—Basketball Jones: Sam Jones' accurate bank shots and .803 free-throw percentage made him a linchpin of Red Auerbach's Boston Celtics in the 1950s and '60s. A fixture of the Bill Russell-Bob Cousy days, Jones was a major factor in the Celts' ten NBA titles during his twelve years with the team. Particularly memorable was the '62 Eastern Division Finals series versus Wilt Chamberlain and the Warriors.

In Game 7, the score was knotted at 107 with two seconds remaining. Jones launched a jumper over Wilt the Stilt—and nailed it for the win. Jones and the Celts went on to defeat the L.A. Lakers in seven to clinch the Celtics' fourth straight NBA title.

1965—"Havlicek Stole the Ball!": It was Game 7 of the Eastern Conference Finals between the defending champion

Boston Celtics and the Philadelphia 76ers. In the waning seconds of the deciding game at Boston Garden, the Celtics were up by a single point, 110 to 109. The Celtics' Bill Russell attempted an inbounds pass, but the ball was deflected by an overhead guywire. The 76ers got the ball with five seconds to play.

The plan was for Sixers guard Hal Greer to inbound the ball to Wilt Chamberlain, but Wilt was covered by Russell. Beyond the key, Sixers forward Chet Walker appeared to be open—but Greer didn't see Boston's John Havlicek, just two steps out of his line of sight, waiting for his opportunity. When Greer released the ball, Havlicek made his move.

Celtics radio announcer Johnny Most called the action—one of the most famous calls in sports history: "Greer is putting the ball into play. . . He gets it out deep. . . Havlicek stole the ball! It's all over! Johnny Havlicek stole the ball!" Over the years, that tape has been replayed countless times, immortalizing a thrilling moment in NBA history.

Basketball is a
game of adversity.
So is life.

A Suffering Busines

CHAPTER 3

Want to know what adversity's all about? Ask Coach Rivers.

Before he turned to coaching, Glenn "Doc" Rivers was one of the most underrated players in the NBA. A big, powerful guard, Doc could slash to the hole like a hot machete through butter. He was the heart and soul of some very good Atlanta Hawks ballclubs in the 1980s, before moving on to the L.A. Clippers, New York Knicks, and San Antonio Spurs. During his thirteen-year career, his teams made it into the postseason ten times (incredibly, even the '92 Clippers made the playoffs with Doc aboard).

It's a tragedy that a player like Doc Rivers has no championship ring to show for everything he has given to the game. His individual performance could prod a middling team into the playoffs—but how could any one player lift a team past Larry Bird and the Celtics or Magic Johnson and the Lakers? It just wasn't gonna happen. So Doc endured thirteen years of intense struggle, adversity, and disappointment.

Doc Rivers has battled adversity since his boyhood. His parents, Grady (a Chicago policeman) and Bettye Rivers, taught him to believe in himself and to dream big dreams. But he had a teacher who once tried to shrink his dreams down to size. Glenn was a third-grader in Maywood, Illinois, and his teacher asked the students to come to the blackboard and write what they planned to be when they grew up. Glenn went to the board, chalk in hand, and wrote, "Professional Basketball Player."

The teacher frowned and told him it was an unrealistic goal. She erased Glenn's words, then told him to write something else—lawyer, doctor, shoe clerk, anything he wanted. Glenn wrote, "Professional Basketball Player." The teacher erased it again, and gave him one more chance. Glenn wrote the same words again, and the teacher sent him to the principal's office.

After hearing the story, the principal sided with Glenn. When they heard about it, so did Grady and Bettye Rivers. In time, Doc Rivers enjoyed a thirteen-year career doing exactly what he said he would do.

Like a Dagger

While at Marquette University in Milwaukee, Doc met Kris, the young lady who would become his wife. Doc is black; Kris is white—and there were some tiny little minds that didn't think black and white belonged together. They underscored their ugly notions by slashing Kris's tires and scrawling hateful epithets on the ground. But Doc and Kris refused to let the hatred of others deter their love.

After his NBA retirement, Doc became an analyst for Turner Broadcasting, teaming up with veteran broadcaster Verne Lundquist. It was in 1997, a year into Doc's broadcast career, that another bunch of tiny minds invaded the lives of Doc and Kris Rivers. They entered the Rivers' Texas home, trashed it, and set it ablaze. Lost in the flames were thirteen years of memorabilia from his NBA career, plus a longtime family friend— a blind dog named Ginger.

"There are no wimps in the Bible. . . . They were very strong, dedicated people that I sort of pattern my life after. They had something they believed in. I don't necessarily join the glee club when I go out to play 48 minutes. I go out for business and one thing only, and that's to get a victory. I don't physically have to go out and fight, but I go out for war, and that's what it's all about. That's what makes it exciting to me."

A. C. GREEN
FORWARD, L.A. LAKERS, PHOENIX SUNS,
DALLAS MAVERICKS, AND MIAMI HEAT

The loss was painful for the whole family. Doc, a father of four, later reflected, "Sometimes, my kids will be talking about some toy, and they'll say, 'Oh, that was in the house that burned.' That's like a dagger through me."

Doc served a three-year stint behind the Turner microphone. He quickly tired of the kind of low-post ball-slogging he saw night after night. He imagined what it would be like to build a team *his* way—a brisk run-and-gun offense, a furious defense forcing turnovers, a fast-break transition game that would run the legs off the opposing teams. In 1999, John Gabriel, general manager of the Orlando Magic, called Doc and offered him the coaching position just vacated by Hall of Famer Chuck Daly—just what Doc had been waiting for.

Coaching the Magic allowed him to work alongside his hero, Julius Erving, now an executive vice-president with the Magic organization. (It was NCAA coach Rick Majerus who hung the "Doc" moniker on Rivers after the young athlete showed up at basketball camp in a "Dr. J" tee shirt.)

Taking over the Magic meant that Doc Rivers would be (to use that despised word) "rebuilding." The team was still reeling from the dismantling

of a stellar lineup that once included Shaquille O'Neal, Penny Hardaway, Horace Grant, and Nick Anderson. But Doc was dead-serious about making the Magic a championship contender once more.

An Aura of Optimism

I vividly recall Doc's first regular season game as coach of the Magic. It was a Friday night, and the Cleveland Cavaliers had come to town. Five minutes before the game, I passed Doc in the tunnel. We chatted briefly, thirty seconds at most. He said, "I heard you and your wife are running in the New York Marathon this Sunday. I wanted to wish you both good luck."

I shook his hand and said, "Have a great season, Coach!"

He grinned, then went out to coach his first pro game. The Magic started strong, blew a 12-point lead, went scoreless from the field for almost 6 minutes down the stretch, and lost 104 to 99. It was a frustrating way to launch the season. The team left right after the game to fly to Washington, D.C., for a game the next night.

The next day, my wife Ruth and I flew to New York and checked into our hotel. We found a basket of fruit waiting for us in the room. On the basket was a card with good wishes from Doc Rivers. I was amazed. Doc and I had only chatted a few seconds in the tunnel, and I hadn't even told him what hotel we were staying in. Even after such a bruising loss, he took the time to find out where Ruth and I were staying, and he showed us that kindness. That speaks volumes about Doc Rivers.

During that first season, Doc put his players through grueling conditioning drills. His goal was to build a team with so much stamina that no other team could outlast them. It worked.

After Detroit Pistons' star forward Grant Hill got a chance to play against the new, improved Orlando Magic, he was awed. "That was a hard team to play," Hill later recalled. He was so impressed that when he became a free agent in 2000, there was only one place he wanted to play: Orlando. After signing with the Magic, Hill told the press, "I thank the Lord for a chance to play in Orlando. This feels like a good fit."

> "Struggle is part of being a man. But if you have faith, there is nothing that can disturb you."
>
> DIKEMBE MUTUMBO
> CENTER, DENVER NUGGETS, ATLANTA HAWKS, AND PHILADELPHIA 76ERS

The chance to play for Doc Rivers also appealed to rising young star Tracy McGrady, unhappy after three years as a bench player with the Toronto Raptors. He, too, was stunned when he faced Doc's revitalized Magic. "We thought we were going to just run all over Orlando," McGrady recalled. "But for them to go out and play hard for 48 minutes just made my decision a lot easier. Doc's a great coach."

There is an aura of optimism that surrounds Doc—not a naive optimism, but the kind of rugged, pragmatic confidence that comes from having conquered adversity. Doc approaches basketball the same way he approaches life: He meets adversity head-on. He runs to it, slashes through it, and *wins*.

Trumped By a Wildcard

Back in 1977-78, when I was general manager of the Philadelphia 76ers, I learned a big lesson in adversity. That year, the Sixers racked up an impressive 55 and 27 record. We went into the play-offs with the fans and sports-writers predicting we would win it all. In the Eastern Conference finals, we faced the wildcard Washington Bullets. Though the Bullets featured some great talent (including Wes Unseld and Elvin Hayes), the Sixers were called "The Best Team Money Can Buy." Our roster boasted Julius Erving, Doug Collins, George McGinnis, Joe Bryant (Kobe's dad), Darryl Dawkins, Lloyd Free, and Caldwell Jones.

The Bullets won Game 1 in Philadelphia and Games 3 and 4 in Washington. The stunned Sixers crawled back to Philly, down three games to one. We won Game 5 at home, then it was back to Washington for Game 6—a hard-fought contest all the way. With less than ten seconds left in regulation play, Washington's Wes Unseld tipped in an offensive rebound, and the Bullets were up by two. The Sixers called a timeout to set up a final play that would send the game into overtime. The plan was to get the ball to Lloyd Free, who would penetrate then dish off to Dr. J. Then the Doctor would perform his usual buzzer-beating magic. Piece of cake.

The play started off as planned—but as Free penetrated the perimeter, elbowing past Elvin Hayes, a whistle blew. Free was ticketed for an offensive foul, possession went to Washington, and the game was sealed. Thus our season ended. We had been trumped by the wildcard Bullets.

I went to the office the following day, and the mood was funereal. No one spoke. Everyone in the office was simply devastated. I slumped behind my desk and tried to work, but I couldn't think of anything but the loss.

I heard footsteps at my door and looked up. There, in the open doorway, was my friend Chuck Daly, our assistant coach. He said one sentence to me: "Ours is a suffering business." Then he turned and was gone.

He had put it so succinctly. Basketball *is* a suffering business. When the season's over, every team is suffering except one. The best teams in the league go into the playoffs—and all but one end their season with a spirit-crushing loss. Only one team gets to celebrate at the end. A suffering business indeed!

Life, too, is a suffering business. We all face adversity. The apostle Paul put it this way: "We are hard pressed on every side, yet not crushed; we are perplexed, but not in despair; persecuted, but not forsaken; struck down, but not destroyed" (2 Cor. 4:8–9). The key to overcoming adversity is to face it with courage, perseverance, and faith in God, who has ultimate control over all our circumstances. As David Robinson says, "If you walk with God, you can have victory—even when things get really tough."

> *"But thanks be to God, who gives us the victory through our Lord Jesus Christ."*
>
> 1 CORINTHIANS 15:57

1970—West Fires and Willis Inspires: Game 3 of the 1970 NBA Finals was tied 100-100 with 13 seconds remaining. Then the Knicks' Dave DeBusschere hit a jumper, putting the Knicks up by two. With three seconds remaining and no timeouts, the Lakers had to inbound from the far end and hit a buzzer-beater—impossible! Lakers guard Jerry West received the inbounds pass from Wilt Chamberlain and fired from deep backcourt—a sixty-foot shot. Amazingly, the ball nestled in the basket to tie the game, leaving the Knicks slackjawed and bug-eyed. In overtime, the Knicks rallied for a 111-108 win. (Under today's rules, West's shot would have been a game-winning three-pointer).

In Game 5, Knicks center Willis Reed went out with a torn thigh muscle. He sat out the loss in Game 6, but refused to miss the deciding game. He took an injection for the pain, then limped onto the court at Madison Square Garden. Though hobbled, Reed scored the first two baskets of the game. They were the only points he contributed to the Knick's 113-99 victory, but his courage inspired the Knicks to their first NBA title.

1971-72—The Streak: The Lakers were the "over-the-hill gang." Elgin Baylor was 37 (with bad knees), Jerry West was 33, and Wilt Chamberlain was 35. But that season, they seemed ageless. On

November 5, 1971, the Lakers beat the Baltimore Bullets, and they kept winning until the Milwaukee Bucks beat them on January 9, 1972—a thirty-three-game streak. The Lakers finished with a then-record sixty-nine-season wins and an NBA championship.

1976—A Boston Marathon:

Game 5 of the 1976 NBA Finals was a triple-overtime thriller at Boston Garden. The Celtics and the Phoenix Suns had split the first four games. With four ticks left in the second OT, Phoenix was up by one—but the Celts' John Havlicek unleashed a fifteen-foot bank shot that found the hole. The fans flooded the court, thinking the game was won, but the officials cleared the floor—there was still one second left to play. Suns guard Paul Westphal shrewdly called a timeout, knowing his team was out of timeouts. The resulting technical foul extended Boston's lead to two, but also gave the Suns the ball at midcourt with a full second to play. The ball was inbounded to Suns forward Garfield Heard, who fired a perfect twenty-foot jumper to force a third overtime. Heard's shot only delayed a Celtics' victory,

128-126, in triple overtime. Boston went on to win Game 6 for the championship.

1978—The Duel: The tightest and most famous scoring shootout in NBA history pitted David Thomson of the Denver Nuggets against George "Iceman" Gervin of the San Antonio Spurs. The rivalry raged throughout the 1977-78 season, culminating on April 9, 1978. It was the last day of the season, and Thompson, playing against Detroit, scored 73 points. Gervin, facing the New Orleans Jazz later that night, knew he had to score 58 to win The Duel. By the end of the game, he had collected 63.

1980—Doc's Greatest Shot: As general manager of the Philadelphia 76ers, I was at courtside for this one, and I still don't believe it. It was Game 4 of the NBA Finals—Julius Erving and the Sixers versus the Lakers for the title. The Lakers were up two games to one. We needed a win at home to even it up. In the fourth quarter, Doc got the ball, beat Lakers forward Mark Landsberger on the right side, and went up for a dunk—but Lakers center Kareem Abdul-Jabbar was there to block him. Doc contorted his body in midair to avoid Kareem, falling out of bounds. With his incredible reach, Doc somehow made a reverse layup as he sailed behind the backboard. Lakers guard Magic Johnson called it "the greatest move I've ever seen." The Sixers won, 105-102, but the Lakers took the series in six.

Say yes to life.
Say yes to your game.
Say no to temptation.

Keep out of Foul Troubl

David Wood was a longtime journeyman in the NBA—not All-Star caliber, perhaps, but certainly a great team player who could always be relied on to fill his role. He enjoyed a long pro career with five NBA teams: the Chicago Bulls, Milwaukee Bucks, and all three Texas teams—the Mavericks, Rockets, and Spurs. His favorite memory was of a shot he made while playing for Houston against the L.A. Clippers. "I got the ball with six seconds left," he recalls. "We were down by three, and I turned and shot a forty-footer that hit nothing but net. That was great."

Known for his physical playing style and tough, scrappy attitude, Wood was a Christian player who portrayed the tough, assertive side of the Christian faith. "I came to the NBA in faith," he told an interviewer. "I thought it was God's will for me to play in the NBA. . . . I worked like it depended on me and I prayed like it depended on God."

Wood's physical and verbal battles with the ultra-aggressive Charles Barkley are legendary. Barkley used to growl, "If the referees call the game right, there's no way David Wood can guard me." Wood always found Barkley's complaints amusing. "I fight like a cornered dog to keep [Barkley] away from the basket," Wood once said. "He really gets frustrated and upset, and then he tries to clobber me."

Wood was always active in NBA chapels, and remains involved with the Fellowship of Christian Athletes (FCA). He also co-founded a basketball evangelism outreach, Jammin' Against the Darkness, with evangelist Steve Jamison. Appearing with NBA players David Robinson, Avery Johnson, A. C. Green, Hersey Hawkins, Andrew Lang, and others, Wood gives basketball demonstrations; talks about his faith in Jesus Christ; and encourages young basketball fans to

keep themselves morally pure and avoid alcohol, tobacco, and drugs. Jammin' rallies have been held in major cities from Seattle (Washington), to New York City to San Juan, Puerto Rico.

"One benefit a Christian has over a non-Christian is you can have self-discipline," he told FCA's *Sharing the Victory* magazine. "You are not a slave to the flesh, but you can be a slave to righteousness and have control. You can say no to drugs. You can say no to premarital sex, you can say no to dating so you can go to the gym and work on your game. You don't have anything that latches hold to you and controls you, as a non-believer would. . . . Put God first and work on your athletic goals."

Abstinence and the Iron Man

Another strong man of faith is A. C. Green. His career has taken him from the L.A. Laker's "Showtime" offense of the late '80s (where he played alongside Magic Johnson, James Worthy, and Kareem Abdul-Jabbar) to the Phoenix Suns (teamed up with Charles Barkley) through a rebulding stint with the Dallas Mavericks. A solid rebounder, an unselfish yet consistent scorer, Green has been a valuable asset to every team he has played on. He ended the 2000-01 season with the Miami Heat and continues the longest iron man streak in NBA history—1,192 consecutive games played.

"If you put yourself in situations of temptation, nine out of ten times you're going to mess up. The key is to put yourself in situations where you won't fall."

HUBERT DAVIS
GUARD, NEW YORK KNICKS, TORONTO
RAPTORS, DALLAS MAVERICKS, AND
WASHINGTON WIZARDS

But A. C. Green's contributions as an NBA player pale compared to everything he contributes to the lives of countless young people. He is a tireless crusader for the Christian faith and Bible-based morality. He proclaims his message of faith and abstinence at youth rallies across the country. He has also developed *A. C. Green's Game Plan Abstinence Program* and the *It Ain't Worth It* video, both of which are used to teach abstinence in public middle schools and high schools around the country.

Most important of all, A. C. practices what he preaches. After sixteen seasons in the NBA (including three NBA championship seasons), Green is unmarried and a self-proclaimed virgin. In our sex-drenched, morally lax society, Green's claim of total abstinence draws reactions ranging from skepticism to ridicule.

"It's an established fact," Green insists. "It's all been scrutinized. Still, the curiosity is always there."

> "There are a lot of temptations out there. The one thing that got me through those things was my Christian faith."
>
> BRIAN SKINNER
> POWER FORWARD,
> L.A. CLIPPERS, CHICAGO BULLS,
> TORONTO RAPTORS

In 1994, Shaquille O'Neal and the Orlando Magic went to Phoenix to play A. C. Green and the Suns. Shaq's low-percentage free throw shooting is legendary, and as usual, he struggled from the line that night. After being fouled, Shaq made one more trip to the line, and A. C. called out to him from the lane, "Hey, Shaq, you'll be all right once you get some experience."

"Yeah," Shaq deadpanned right back at him, "and you'll be okay once *you* get some."

It was a funny jab, and Green took it with a grin. But he is dead serious about the importance of avoiding temptation and remaining pure. "Opportunities for temptation come and go," he says, "but by the grace of God, I will hold myself sexually abstinent until I marry. I am single, and I have a wonderful girlfriend. For me, abstinence is more than a statement. It's a personal conviction."

"A. C. has a deep, deep belief born out of his faith," says Pat Riley, who coached Green with both the Lakers and the Heat. "He knows who he is as a man. His reality can't be threatened by anybody's insincere comments or anybody's ignorance. He laughs at it and moves beyond all that."

That's A. C. Green—the steadfast iron man. Some people would say you'd *have* to be made of iron to maintain a life of sexual abstinence well into your thirties, as A. C. has done. But he says it is not a matter of an iron will. It's simply a matter of faith and a genuine love for God.

"I've stuck to it," he says, "but it's only been by God's grace. I keep looking to Him to be my source and power. But at the same time, I keep looking to Him because I love Him, I want to please Him, and I want to be committed to Him."

Winning the Crown of Life

Green doesn't worry about the scorn and ridicule he often faces as a Christian living righteously in a sin-sick world. But he worries about kids today who are pressured by a society that tells them they are not cool unless they are promiscuous. "Sexual abstinence is one of the most unpopular things you can do," says A. C., "but society hasn't given any better alternatives. Telling kids that condoms are the best way to get involved sexually with somebody is wrong."

What society calls "safe sex" or "safer sex" is nothing but a deadly game of sexual roulette. "The idea that's spread," says Green, "is that kids are going to have sex, so everyone should adjust and get them 'safer' sex. Personally, I don't think young people are being given the whole truth. They're being force-fed a lot of lies about sexual behavior and 'safe sex.' These lies are cutting down kids in the prime of their lives. Lies

are destroying the dreams of college and career, and at times, taking the very lives of these kids through deadly diseases."

A. C. knows that kids don't have to choose between promiscuous sex and the risk of so-called "safe sex." There is a third alternative that he calls *saved sex*—sex that is saved until marriage. That is the only truly healthy option. He knows it works because he lives it every day, amid the intense temptations that come his way as a professional athlete. He has money, fame, opportunity, and enormous temptation for pride and arrogance. Amid such temptation, there is only one way that A. C. Green can keep himself pure—and it's the same way that he advocates to young people and older people alike: Faith in God, and reliance upon the power of Jesus Christ.

The Bible is God's game plan, and it tells us how to keep out of foul trouble. The apostle Paul tells us that the best way to beat temptation is to steer clear of enticing situations—

to literally flee or run away from situations we might not be able to handle. "Flee sexual immorality," Paul writes. "Every sin that a man does is outside the body, but he who commits sexual immorality sins against his own body" (1 Cor. 6:18).

Some people rationalize their sin, saying, "I just can't help myself. The temptation I face is too great. Abstinence is just impossible for me." Again, the apostle Paul answers, "No temptation has overtaken you except such as is common to man; but God is faithful, who will not allow you to be tempted beyond what you are able, but with the temptation will also make the way of escape, that you may be able to bear it" (1 Cor. 10:13).

What's more, the Bible puts the issue of temptation into terms that any basketball fan can understand: Those who play by God's rules and keep out of foul trouble can expect to win a championship—what the Bible calls "the crown of life." As James 1:12 tells us, "Blessed is the man who endures temptation; for when he has been approved, he will receive the crown of life which the Lord has promised to those who love Him."

1981—The Boss of the Hardwood: Early in his career, Larry Bird was in a Dallas watering hole with Boston Globe reporter Dan Shaughnessy. Glancing out the front window, Bird saw scores of young people hurrying past. "Where are all those kids going?" he asked.

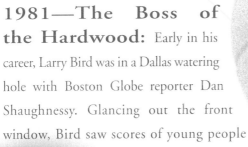

"There's a Springsteen concert down the street," said Shaughnessy.

"Who's Springsteen?" asked Bird.

"Who's Springsteen!" said the astonished reporter. "You really never heard of Bruce Springsteen? The guy they call The Boss?"

Bird shook his head. "Who is he?"

"Larry," said Shaughnessy, "he's the you of rock and roll."

Then Bird understood. "The guy must be pretty good then."

No question, Larry Bird was The Boss of the Hardwood. In 1981, in his second NBA season, Bird took Boston to an NBA championship. The most electrifying moment of the '81 Finals came during Game 1 between the Celtics and the Houston Rockets at Boston Garden.

In the fourth quarter, Bird launched an eighteen-foot jump shot from the right side. Before the ball cleared his fingertips, Bird knew he had missed—but he calculated that it would deflect to the right and he dashed for the spot where the ball would arrive. Snatching the rebound on the run, he switched the ball to his left hand, making a humanly impossible layup as he fell out of bounds. The crowd went wild—and the Celtics went on to win the game, and later the championship.

"Watch and pray, lest you enter into temptation. The spirit indeed is willing, but the flesh is weak."

MATTHEW 26:41

1983—Raining Buckets:

On December 13, the Denver Nuggets hosted the Detroit Pistons for a triple-OT shootout, the highest-scoring game in NBA history. Guard Isiah Thomas was the top-scoring Piston with 47 points; he was topped by Denver forward Kiki Vandeweghe, who scored 51. Denver won, 186-184.

1984—The Skyhook: On April 5, Kareem Abdul-Jabbar and the Lakers trekked to Vegas to play the Utah Jazz and make NBA

history. Kareem received a pass from Magic Johnson, did a 180, and put up his patented skyhook—nothing but net. That shot gave Kareem the 31,420th point of his career, elevating him above Wilt Chamberlain as the NBA's all-time scorer. By his 1989 retirement, Abdul-Jabbar had 38,387 career points.

1984—The Clothesline: In the 1984 NBA Finals, the Lakers and Celtics—bitter rivals—split the first two games. In Game 3, Magic Johnson and the Lakers annihilated the Celts, 137-104. After the loss, Celtics forward Larry Bird berated his team: "We played like sissies out there!" In Game 4, fired by Bird's reprimand, Celtics forward Kevin McHale came out and clotheslined Lakers forward Kurt Rambis while Rambis drove on a breakaway. McHale's attack ignited a brawl on the floor—but it also swung the momentum of the series. The Celts won the title in seven.

1987—The Steal:

In Game 5 of the Eastern Conference Finals at Boston Garden, the legendary Celtics faced the brash young Detroit Pistons. By the fourth quarter, the Pistons had battled back from a 12-point deficit. With seconds remaining, Isiah Thomas put the Pistons on top by one with a seventeen-foot jumper. Boston's Larry Bird took the ball downcourt to work the baseline, but was rejected by a young Dennis Rodman (pre-tattoos, pre-DayGlo® hair). The ball deflected out of bounds off Boston's Jerry Sichting. Possession: Detroit. Time remaining: five ticks. Wanting an inbounds from mid-court, Pistons coach Chuck Daly hollered, "Time out!" Isiah Thomas didn't hear Daly, and lobbed an inbounds pass toward Bill Laimbeer at the hole. Noting the ball's lazy trajectory, Bird leaped, snagged the ball, and passed to teammate Dennis Johnson for the lay-in. Boston won, 108-107. The Celts captured the series in seven to advance to the Finals, where they fell to the Lakers in six.

*To be a champion
in the game of life,
you've got to win on
your own home court.*

The Home Court

His full name is Dikembe Mutombo Mpolondo Mukamba Jean Jacque Wamutombo. No wonder his team-mates call him "Deke." His big name befits a big man with a big heart. When you know his story, you can easily see why the *Sporting News* named him Good Guy of the Year in their annual poll for the 2000-01 season.

The 7' 2" center for the Philadelphia 76ers is one of the most dominant defenders in the NBA (he previously played with the Denver Nuggets and Atlanta Hawks). Selected NBA Defensive Player of the Year in 1995, '97, '98, and 2001, Mutombo has towered as a shot-blocker and rebounder throughout his decade-long career in the league. He led the NBA in shot-blocking for five consecutive seasons (1993-94 through 1997-98).

Dikembe Mutombo grew up in the Congo (formerly Zaire). Over twenty people lived in his house. His father, a Sorbonne-educated school administrator earning $37 a month, was a generous man who was always helping people. "Helping other people is a tradition in my family," says Mutombo. "My dad always believed that when you have wealth, you should share it with other people."

Mutombo lives out his father's tradition in a big way. For example, he paid for uniforms and travel expenses so that the women's basketball team from his homeland could compete in the 1996 Olympic Games in Atlanta. Even more importantly, he created the

Dikembe Mutombo Foundation (www.dmf.org) to provide humanitarian aid to the people of his African homeland. In 1999, he donated $3.5 million toward a new hospital, hospital beds, and medical supplies in the Congo.

The new hospital, scheduled for completion in 2004, will be the first built in the Congo in four decades. It will be named the Biamba Mutombo Hospital after Dikembe's mother, who died from a probable stroke in 1998. Tragically, this was in the early days of a bloody civil war in the Congo, and the city of Kinshasa was under a military curfew. Anyone on the streets risked being shot, so Dikembe's father could not take Biamba to the hospital for treatment. "She would be alive today," Dikembe reflects with both sadness and anger, "if not for the war."

Biamba Mutombo was just one of an estimated three million people who died in the civil war. When his mother died, Dikembe tried to get a visa to return to Kinshasa from the United States, but his request was denied because of the civil war.

It's hard for Dikembe to discuss his mother's death without emotion. Though he grieves, he knows he will see her again in eternity. As a child, Dikembe Mutombo was steeped in the Christian faith of his mother and father, which includes a belief in the reality of heaven and eternal life. Today, he is passing that same faith down to his own children.

Dikembe and his wife, Rose, are parents to six children. They adopted the first four (two boys, two girls) after his brother died. Their two birth children are a daughter, Carrie Biamba Wamutumbo, and a baby boy, Jean Jacques Dikembe Mutumbo Mplombo Jr. Their top priority as parents is to follow the biblical admonition, "Train up a child in the way he should go, and when he is old he will not depart from it" (Prov. 22:6).

> "The big reason I am the way I am is because of the Lord. I was brought up in a Christian home. My parents are my biggest inspiration. They helped lead us in the right directions."
>
> CHARLIE WARD
> GUARD, NEW YORK KNICKS

> *"Being a Christian has helped develop a close relationship between my wife and me. It's developed a close relationship with my boys, because they know that Dad loves the Lord and puts the Lord first."*
>
> HERSEY HAWKINS
> GUARD, SEATTLE SUPERSONICS,
> CHICAGO BULLS, PHILADELPHIA 76ERS,
> CHARLOTTE HORNETS

Like his father, Dikembe Mutombo is passionate on the subject of education. That passion is demonstrated by his two earned degrees in Linguistics and Diplomacy from Georgetown, and his fluency in English, Spanish, Portuguese, French, and five African dialects. Every day, he works to pass this same love of learning along to his kids. "Every day we talk about school," he says, "because a good education is a primary goal with us. Without an education, you can't get anywhere."

He is also passionate about the importance of Christian education through the church. "As a child," he reflects, "I was forced to be in church on Sunday. It was something we knew as an obligation. Now, I choose to go, and I try to translate to my children the importance of going to church."

Dikembe Mutombo recognizes that his most important responsibility is to the "home team," his wife Rose and his six kids. For all his accomplishments on the hardwood, "Deke" Mutombo knows that to be a champion, you've got to win on your own home court.

A Family of Faith

Denny Price was a former NBA assistant coach (Phoenix Suns) who had just joined the coaching staff of the Oklahoma Storm of the United States Basketball League. The father of former four-time NBA All-Star Mark Price and current NBA guard Brent Price, Denny and his sons were putting on a basketball clinic at the YMCA in their

hometown of Enid, Oklahoma. Denny watched his sons put on a one-on-one exhibition, then he stepped onto the court to join them. He fed the ball to Mark, who knocked down a perfect three-pointer, then passed the ball to Brent, who hit a long jumper.

Suddenly, Denny Price staggered, unable to catch his breath. Ken Rapp, executive director of the Enid Family YMCA, was just a few steps from Denny. "Wait a minute," Denny said, grimacing— then he collapsed and Rapp caught him and lowered him to the floor. Rapp performed CPR on Denny until the paramedics arrived to take him to the hospital. A short time later, the father of Mark and

Brent Price was pronounced dead of a heart attack at age sixty-two. "If Denny were going to choose how he wanted to go," said Rapp, "I'd bet it would have been playing basketball with his boys."

Denny's death was a devastating loss for Mark and Brent and their younger brother Matt (a college basketball standout who pursued a non-NBA career). But they were raised by believing parents who taught them to trust God, even in the tragic moments in life. This consolation has taken them through this time of loss: "For if we

believe that Jesus died and rose again, even so God will bring with Him those who sleep in Jesus" (1 Thess. 4:14).

Brent reflects that one of the great lessons his father taught him was *trusting the Lord.* This holds true whether on the basketball court or in the valley of the shadow of death itself. "God's in control," says Brent. "God, in His sovereignty, is more powerful than anything. . . . I wonder how people do it without God."

The Price family has always been close-knit. Denny and his sons founded the Price Family Basketball Camp, which teaches not only the fundamentals of basketball, but the essentials of the Christian faith and biblical values. Denny lived his life as a testimony to others of what eternal life through Jesus Christ is all about. "When we profess to be Christians," he once told *Sharing the Victory* magazine, "it's our responsibility to live it. But it's not like some big obstacle. Christians should never feel like they *have* to witness for Christ, but *want* to."

Denny's enthusiasm for sharing Christ with others has been handed down to his sons. "The Bible calls us all to be a witness for Christ," says Brent, a veteran of the Washington Bullets, Houston Rockets, and Vancouver Grizzlies, who shares the NBA record for the most three-pointers made in a row: thirteen. "When you live in a house made of glass, you're always open to the public. So it's even more important to walk and talk the Christian life."

Almost as important as the faith that Denny Price has passed down to his sons is his commitment to family. Mark learned from his father that family comes ahead of career, ahead of fame, ahead of basketball. Mark's accomplishments in the game—twelve NBA seasons, four All-Star appearances, and a gold medal with Dream Team II—left many wondering why he walked away from the NBA when he clearly had a lot of game left in him. Answer: Family. "I probably could have played longer," says Mark Price, "but we had four kids and the travel was hard."

Denny Price has passed on a legacy of faith and family to his three sons. They learned from a great Christian coach that the most important responsibility any man has is to the "home team." Denny Price taught it and lived it until his very last breath.

Passing It On

LaPhonso Ellis is a veteran center-forward of the Denver Nuggets, Atlanta Hawks, and Minnesota Timberwolves. But even more importantly, Ellis is a Christian, a loving husband to his wife Jennifer, and a committed father to his daughter Elexis and sons LaPhonso Jr. and Walter. It isn't always easy balancing these roles.

"One major obstacle I face," says Ellis, "is just trying to find a balance for my family, for the Lord, and for our responsibilities with me as a professional ballplayer. It's kind of difficult, and things can get out of balance. You start spending too much time in one area, and the balance starts to slip. I think it's a constant juggling act, and we pray to Him when things start to get out of whack."

Another veteran of the hardwood who keeps faith, family, and career in proper balance is Paul Westphal. A fiercely competitive guard, Westphal was a key factor in the Boston Celtics 1974 NBA championship; in 1976, he led the Phoenix Suns to the NBA Finals. The latter years of his twelve-season career were marred by a serious stress fracture, requiring metal pins in his leg. But for five years in Phoenix in the early '80s, he was a basketball force to be reckoned with. In more recent years, he has served exciting, controversial coaching stints with the Phoenix Suns and Seattle SuperSonics.

Yet Paul Westphal also took time to serve as an unpaid basketball coach at Scottsdale Chaparral High, where his son, Michael, was on the team. "I got the same thrills at Chaparral," he recalled, "as I did coaching the Suns. . . . How many guys in this business get to see their sons play even one game? I saw them all. I'll never forget that."

Westphal's wife, Cindy, says that her husband always finds time for his kids, even at the most unlikely moments. On one occasion during a game, Coach Westphal was diagramming a play for his team during a crucial timeout. There was a tug on his arm. Westphal looked down and saw Michael—who was seven at the time—looking up at him. Not a word was said between father and son. Westphal reached into his pocket, pulled out a dollar bill, and handed it to the boy, who took off for the soda stand. Westphal went back to his clipboard and his game.

> *"And you, fathers, do not provoke your children to wrath, but bring them up in the training and admonition of the Lord."*
>
> EPHESIANS 6:4

Paul and Cindy Westphal have been active with a Phoenix-area adoption agency, Christian Family Care. To reduce the number of abortions, the organization helps women with crisis pregnancies place their babies with willing families.

"It seems like the Lord always sends somebody to give these kids a Christian home," says Westphal. "That's why the agency exists."

Paul Westphal credits his parents with building a strong commitment to faith and family into him and his brother Bill. Their dad was a role model who lived out the reality of the Christian faith on a daily basis. Paul and Bill Westphal founded the Westphal Brothers Basketball Camp as a way of "passing it on," combining the principles of the Bible and the fundamentals of basketball to influence and change young lives. Paul Westphal is leaving a legacy, not only for his son Michael and daughter Victoria, but for hundreds of other young people.

A Homecoming Feast

In early June of 2000, Julius Erving called and told me that his son, Cory, was missing. On May 28, the nineteen-year-old had driven his car away from the Erving's Orlando home to buy bread for a Memorial Day cookout. He had not returned. Julius, who has been a friend of mine since we were both with the 76ers, was about to go public about Cory's disappearance. He asked me to serve as the family spokesperson.

Cory had led a troubled life. Afflicted with dyslexia and attention deficit disorder, in and out of drug rehab several times since age fourteen, Cory was thought by some to be just one more runaway among many. Yet, at the time of his disappearance, Cory had turned his life around. He had enrolled at a junior college and had a job at a nearby restaurant. His relationship with his parents was good. Why would he run away?

Julius put up a
$25,000 reward
and made a national
appeal for help, including a June 23
appearance on CNN's *Larry King Live*. He
affectionately described his son to Larry
King, saying, "He has a lot of potential as a
person. He's charming, he's clever, he's kind
of kooky at times. That is the side of Cory
our family knows, and wants the public to
know. So when we make our public plea,
we're not appealing for help in bringing back
a person who is in a downward spiral, who's
down and out. We want the public to help us
bring back a person we love very much, who
can make a contribution to society, and
who is trying to turn his life around."

Larry King took calls from viewers, and
one caller asked how Julius, his wife
Turquoise, and the Erving family were
handling the crisis. "Well, I'll tell you,"
Julius replied, "we're all doing well
under the circumstances. We really
appreciate all the prayers people
have offered. I've been holding

dear to my heart the Scriptures, in particular Luke 15:11, the parable of the prodigal son. That passage says that, in the end, we will all celebrate because our son was lost and now is found. When our son comes home, we'll have a feast and a celebration."

On Thursday, July 6, Seminole County Sheriff Don Eslinger's deputies were combing a retention pond when they came across Cory's black 1999 Volkswagen Passat, submerged under eight feet of water. Cory's body was inside. He had not run away. He had not met with foul play. He had lost his life in a tragic accident.

Immediately after Cory was found, I talked to Julius and offered to help him put out a press release to the media. He dictated a brief statement, in which he said, "I would like to thank Sheriff Eslinger and his staff for returning our son to us."

The lost son had returned home. And after Cory's funeral, just as Julius had promised on *Larry King Live*, the Ervings held a feast for family and friends to celebrate the return of a much-loved son.

Like Dikembe Mutombo, the Price family, LaPhonso Ellis, and Paul Westphal, Julius Erving is a Christian, a husband, and a father above all else. Like the loving father in the story of the prodigal son, he would do anything, go any place, spend any amount for the good of his family. What about you and me? Do we have our priorities straight? As long as it's God and family ahead of everything else, we'll never go wrong.

If we want to be champions in the game of life, we've got to be winners at home.

The Michael Jordan Era:

Seven-year NBA veteran Jim Les (Utah Jazz, Los Angeles Clippers, Sacramento Kings) told me about his encounters with Michael Jordan. "I was a rookie with Utah," he said, "and we were playing the Bulls at home. Early in the game, there was a long rebound, which I scooped up. I headed for the basket, thinking I had an easy layup. From out of nowhere, Jordan was there and blocked it from behind. That led to a quick Bulls basket. A photographer got a good shot of the play just before the block, and he gave it to me.

"Two years later, I was with Sacramento, and the Bulls came to town. At the shoot-around, I asked Michael to sign the photo, which he did. Later that season, we went to Chicago and the same play happened— a long rebound which I got and then took off for a layup. Again, Michael blocked it and knocked me to the floor. While I was down, yelling at the referee for a call, M. J. grinned down at me and said, 'I'll sign that one, too!'"

No other player in NBA history so completely owned an era as did the fabulous Michael Jordan.

1989—The Shot:

On May 7, 1989, Jordan fired "The Shot" heard 'round the world. It was the deciding game in a tight opening-round playoff series. With three seconds left, the Cavaliers' Craig Ehlo had put his team up by one, beating Bulls defender Craig Hodges. In the timeout huddle, Hodges was down on himself. "Don't worry," Jordan told Hodges, "I'm gonna hit the shot." From the right side, Jordan worked toward the key and went up for an inside-the-circle jumper. Ehlo leaped to block it—but as gravity pulled Ehlo back to earth, Jordan seemed to float miraculously in midair. He released The Shot, the buzzer sounded, and the ball sailed home as if it knew the way. The Bulls won, 101-100, knocking the Cavs out of the playoffs.

1991-1992-1993—Bulls' First Three-Peat:

The 1990-91 season established the Bulls dynasty. After sweeping Detroit in the playoffs, Michael Jordan and the Bulls faced Magic Johnson and the Lakers in the NBA Finals. In Game 2, June 5, 1991, Jordan raced down the lane as Lakers

defender Sam Perkins moved to block his shot. Jordan launched himself, switched the ball to his left hand in mid-flight, torqued his body to avoid charging Perkins, and kissed the ball off the glass for two. The

defining image of the '91 Finals shows Michael weeping and embracing both the title trophy and his father.

In 1992, the Bulls beat the Portland Trailblazers four games to two for the repeat. Memorable moment: Michael hitting six treys in the first half of Game 1; after number six, he ran past the TV cameras with his hands spread as if to say, "I can't believe it either!"

The 1993 Finals was a tight see-saw contest versus Charles Barkley and the Phoenix Suns. Chicago took Games 1 and 2 in Phoenix. Game 3 was a triple-OT Phoenix win. In Game 4, Jordan scored 55 points to clinch a 111-105 victory. In Game 5, the Bulls lost at home. In Game 6, the Bulls blew a big lead, going scoreless for over six minutes in the fourth. The Suns were up by two when a 24-second violation gave the ball to the Bulls with 14.1 ticks remaining. Jordan took the ball upcourt, then passed to Scottie Pippen, who passed to Horace Grant at the baseline, who dished out to John Paxson beyond the three-point circle. Paxson spotted up and shot the most perfect three-pointer of his career. Up by one with 3.9 seconds to play, the Bulls stopped the Suns' desperation drive and completed their championship three-peat.

1994—It's Miller Time: It was Indiana Pacers versus the Knicks in Game 5 of the 1994 Eastern Conference Finals. The series was tied 2 and 2. Playing in Madison Square Garden, the Pacers' Reggie Miller got into an uncanny scoring rhythm—39 points in the game, 25 in the fourth quarter alone (including 5 treys). Miller powered a Pacers rally that dismantled the Knicks on their own floor, 93-86. Though the Knicks later won the series in seven, fans will always remember "Miller Time"—twelve wondrous minutes when Reggie couldn't miss.

1996-1997-1998—Bulls' Second Three-Peat: In the 1995-96 season, Jordan and the Bulls won seventy-two regular season games, exploding the 1971-72 Lakers' record of 69. They dismantled the Seattle SuperSonics in six in the Finals. Jordan was MVP for the season, the All-Star Game, and the Finals.

In the 1997 Finals, a dehydrated, flu-weakened Jordan trudged into Game 5—then put on an unforgettable show. Many consider this

Michael's finest hour. Facing the Utah Jazz in Salt Lake City, M. J. knocked down 38 points, including a tie-breaking trey with 25 seconds remaining. The Bulls won, 90 to 88, then clinched the title at home in Game 6, 90 to 86.

The 1998 Finals was a Bulls-Jazz rematch. The defining moment came in the closing seconds of Game 6. With 37 seconds remaining, the Bulls trailed by three. Jordan scored on a layup to bring his team within one. Utah's Karl Malone got the ball with 20 seconds left, only to get stripped by Jordan at the defensive end. When Jordan faked a drive to the hole, Jazz defender Bryon Russell bit on it, leaving Jordan an open shot. With 5.2 seconds left, Jordan buried a twenty-foot jumper. With that shot, the Bulls claimed an 87-86 victory—and their second championship three-peat.

Want to take your game above the rim? Then practice your vertical leap.

Above the Rim

In the summer of 1978, early in my tenure as general manager of the Philadelphia 76ers, we made a major trade, sending George McGinnis to the Denver Nuggets for 6' 9" forward Bobby Jones. A versatile sixth man and probably the most underrated and unselfish player ever to play the game, Bobby was a big factor in getting the Sixers a championship in 1983. More than that, he brought a potent moral and spiritual influence to the Sixers.

The lanky Charlotte native never drank, smoked, or swore. Honored by Seagram Distillers with a $10,000 prize for the Most Consistent and Productive Player, he donated the money to religious charities rather than benefit personally from whiskey profits. I only recall one time Bobby ever argued with an official. The ref had called a foul on one of Bobby's teammates, and Bobby politely told him, "Sir, that foul was on me."

Bobby Jones was a solid offensive player and one of the toughest defenders in the game, yet he played a clean, honest game—no elbow-throwing or hip-checking. The Sixers never missed the playoffs while Bobby was on the team. He was a tireless worker, unfailingly courteous, and unbelievably humble. He'd pour his blood and sweat out on the floor for 48 minutes, then shower and go home. If you ask me to name one NBA player that a kid should model his life after, it would be Bobby, hands down. Charles Barkley (who, as a rookie, was a Sixers teammate of Bobby's) once said, "If everyone in the world was like Bobby Jones, the world wouldn't have any problems."

Bobby attributed his intense work ethic to Colossians 3:23: "And what-ever you do, do it heartily, as to the Lord and not to men." During our championship season, he told *NBA Today,* "When I'm in there, I just play as hard as I can. In the Bible, it says we're supposed to give 100 percent in whatever it is we do, and that's what I do." That attitude earned him eight selections to the NBA All-Defensive First Team, four NBA All-Star appearances, and a championship ring. Despite health problems that included an irregular heartbeat, asthma, and epilepsy, Bobby enjoyed a successful twelve-year career.

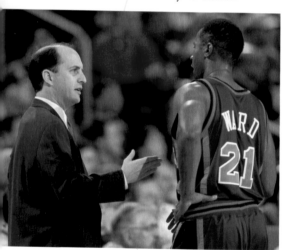

Bobby's Bold Idea

Though he had a quiet demeanor, Bobby Jones absolutely pulsated with Christian fervor and love for God. There were not many subjects that he spoke about in a passionate way—not even basketball. But when he talked about Jesus, his eyes came alight and his voice and gestures became animated. One of the first things Bobby did when he joined the Sixers was to approach me with a brand-new concept: pre-game chapels. I thought it was a terrific idea.

So the first NBA chapel was held in February 1979, before a game against the Milwaukee Bucks at Philadelphia's Spectrum Arena.

Our speaker was Melvin Floyd, an African-American youth worker from inner-city Philadelphia. Three players showed up—Bobby, Julius Erving, and Milwaukee's Kent Benson—plus assistant coach Chuck Daly. Then as now, the time allotted for the chapel service was short—about twelve minutes. Despite the small size of his congregation, Mel got so wound up that I had to go in and tell him it was time to close because the game was starting. From that small and inauspicious start, the practice of team chapel services has spread throughout the NBA—and they can be all traced back to Bobby Jones.

Of course, not everyone is a fan of NBA chapels. Knicks head coach Jeff Van Gundy made a big stir when he told an interviewer for *New York* magazine that the two worst things to happen to the NBA were God and golf. Referring to the Knicks longtime chaplain, Pastor John Love, Van Gundy said, "We've given this guy too much freedom. He spends

> *"When I gave my life to Jesus Christ, I began to understand my true purpose for being here. . . . The purpose of life is to be found through having Christ in your life, understanding what His plan is, and following that plan. . . . Since I asked Christ to be my Lord and Savior, there are still some peaks and valleys. But I am being operated on by the greatest Doctor of them all, so the glory goes to Him."*
>
> JULIUS ERVING (DR. J)
> FORWARD, VIRGINIA SQUIRES (ABA),
> NEW YORK NETS (ABA),
> AND PHILADELPHIA 76ERS (NBA)

as much time as he wants with our players before games. Do people in offices have preachers coming into their place of business, interrupting their work?"

Van Gundy apparently forgot that one of his toughest, most physical players is Charlie Ward, a dedicated Christian and loyal chapel attendee. "Chapel has never been a distraction for me, and it never will be," Ward responded. "It's my ritual."

With the Orlando Magic, we know that pre-game chapel services are not a distraction. They help our players get focused and ready to play. We usually have six to twelve guys from both teams in our chapel services. We find that, in the pressure-packed, temptation-charged world of pro sports, Bobby Jones' inspired idea provides a beacon of light, an island of stability, so that these guys can go out and compete with intensity.

Read the Instruction Manual

They call him The Admiral, because he is a product of the Naval Academy. I call him The *Admirable* Admiral, because he has given a generation of young sports fans so much to admire and emulate. Center David Robinson of the San Antonio Spurs has had a legendary basketball career: Robinson represented the U.S.A. in three Olympics (1988, '92, '96), won an NBA championship in '99, and was selected as one of the fifty greatest players in NBA history. But even more admirable is his commitment to his Christian faith and moral values.

Sports Illustrated seemed shocked that any NBA player could be as morally upright and spiritually strong as David Robinson. "The Silver Dancers come onto the court during a timeout, and David Robinson does not watch," marveled *SI* writer Leigh Montville. "The Silver Dancers are the Spurs' version of the Laker Girls, choreographed for the maximum number of jiggles and pelvic thrusts. Their uniform tonight is hot pants and tight silver shirts. . . . No, David Robinson does not watch. . . . He is a Christian."

Robinson stands 7' 1" tall, and from that altitude, he proudly proclaims Jesus Christ as his Lord and Savior. He calls June 8, 1991—the day he gave his life to Christ—"my second birthday." By that time, he was already an NBA All-Star (he was the number one selection in the 1987 NBA draft). Raised by Christian parents, he was obligated to attend church most of his life but had never been interested in matters of faith and Christian living. "My mother was a Christian," Robinson recalls, "and I always figured I'm a Christian because she's a Christian— a family thing."

> *"When you accept Jesus, you've won the championship."*
>
> ALLAN HOUSTON
> GUARD, NEW YORK KNICKS

One day, evangelist Greg Ball of Champions for Christ came to the Spurs' locker room to talk about Jesus. Robinson tried to put him off, but Ball was persistent. Finally Robinson agreed to give him a few minutes and told Ball to come by his house.

Greg Ball arrived and they sat down to talk. He asked Robinson, "Do you really love God?"

"Sure, I love Him," answered The Admiral.

"How much time do you spend reading your Bible and praying?"

"Not much."

"When you love someone," said Ball, "don't you want to spend time getting to know that person?"

"I suppose so," said Robinson.

"In the Old Testament," said Ball, "God said, 'Take one day a week and honor Me.' When was the last time you took one day and honored God?"

"A whole day!" said Robinson. "I don't think I've ever spent a whole day praising God. I mean I've gone to church before—but never a whole day."

David Robinson later reflected on that moment and recalled, "That just broke my heart. I realized that here's God, the most incredible Person in my life and I've never once thanked Him, never honored Him. I felt like a spoiled brat. I got on my knees and cried. I said, 'Lord, from this day forward I'm going to spend as much time as I can getting to know You, learning about You, and learning how to love You.'"

After that, he recalls, "I was a different person. Everybody in my life could see the change. . . . When your heart really is broken and you realize that God deserves everything, you need to talk to Him with that broken heart and say, 'Lord, I have sinned. Please forgive me for my sins and let me start all over. Give me new life through the forgiveness of Jesus Christ.'"

Greg Ball gave Robinson a Bible, calling it "the instruction manual for living." Well, Robinson loved to put things together—he once built a big-screen TV from a kit—so he knew it was important to follow the instructions. He began reading that Bible—and in the process, he began reassembling his life.

"I'd always told myself I was a good guy, no matter what I'd done," Robinson reflected. But the

Bible told him a different story: "As it is written: 'There is none righteous, no, not one' . . . for all have sinned and fall short of the glory of God" (Rom. 3:10, 23). That's the bad news. Here's the good news: "For the wages of sin is death, but the gift of God is eternal life in Christ Jesus our Lord" (Rom. 6:23).

A week after his conversation with Greg Ball, David Robinson was baptized. Three months later, in September 1991, he proposed to a Christian young woman named Valerie. He had dated her for a while, then had broken up with her. After he gave his life to Christ, he couldn't stop thinking about her. "I called her and told her how I'd been reading the Bible," he recalled. "She was the same sweet, wonderful person she had been before and is now. I just hadn't been paying attention." They were married a short time later, and they now have three sons, David, Corey, and Justin.

A Magic Walk

For some reason, Christians in physical sports such as football and basketball are often labeled "soft," even when all the stats and highlight film show otherwise. One media pundit will raise it, others will jump on it, and after enough repetitions, some fans will start to believe it. This kind of talk, which is based on media misconceptions of what Christianity is all about, has dogged David Robinson despite the fact that he has been the NBA's top scorer, a league MVP, and has always had some of the highest rebounding and shot-blocking stats in the league. You don't rack up these accomplishments by being "soft."

Robinson scored 71 points against the Clippers on the final day of the 1993-94 season (the year he was the NBA's top scorer, averaging 29.8 points per game). In his twelfth NBA season, 2000-01, he appeared in 80 games (fighting severe back pain), and averaged 14.4 points, 8.6 rebounds, and 2.46 blocks per game. He scored 20 or more points 11 times, scored in double figures 67 times, achieved 22 double-doubles, blocked 4 or more shots 18 times with a season-high 8 rejections on March 22 at Atlanta. He recorded his 19,000th career point on

March 9 against the Lakers in L.A. That is not the resumé of a "soft" player.

Robinson plays clean, but he plays physical—and he attributes his power and physical prowess on the court to his Christian values. "I'm not playing for the fans or the money, but to honor God," he told *Sports Illustrated.* "I know my motivation. I know where I'm headed. Every night I try to go out there to honor Him and play great."

David Robinson is a man of diverse talents. He has a keen mind, having earned a degree in mathematics from the Naval Academy (he scored 1320 out of a possible 1600 on the SAT). As a boy, he would accompany his mother to the grocery store and would total the price of her purchases in his head before they reached the checkout stand. At age fourteen, he was taking advanced computer courses at a local college. He taught himself to play jazz and classical piano (he owns a baby grand and takes a keyboard on road trips), as well as the saxophone. He is also a gifted public speaker. His father, Ambrose, predicts that David could well be the next Billy Graham after he retires from the game.

Robinson sums up his life with Christ in a single sentence: "I found the Lord, and since then everything has been like a magic walk." David Robinson lives his life above the rim— thanks to his vertical leap. No, I'm not talking about his dunking, his shot-blocking, or his vertical leap on the basketball court. I'm talking about the vertical leap he took when he said yes to Jesus Christ—a vertical leap of faith. It's a leap anyone can take. The Admiral has taken that leap. So has the great Bobby Jones. So have I.

> *"I press toward the goal for the prize of the upward call of God in Christ Jesus."*
>
> PHILIPPIANS 3:14

And so can you. Once you take that leap, you just keep going higher and higher, and you never come down. So live your life above the rim, my friend. Make sure you take that vertical leap of faith.

The Maravich Mystique

Remembering Pistol Pete

Beginning in 1969, I spent four years as general manager of the Chicago Bulls, then moved to Atlanta as general manager of the Hawks in 1973. During my four years in Chicago, we made the playoffs each year. But during my single season in Atlanta, losing was the norm. We lost sixteen of our first seventeen road games after New Year's Day. We called back-to-back wins a "streak." I was baffled because we had good players—Lou Hudson, Walt Hazzard, Walt Bellamy, and the great Pistol Pete Maravich—plus a brilliant coach, Cotton Fitzsimmons. But the team just couldn't win games.

Cotton hated to lose, and he tried to psych up his players every which way. Nothing worked. One night, he focused his pregame pep talk on the word *pretend*. "Fellas," he said, "I want you to *pretend* that you're the greatest basketball team in the world. And I want you to *pretend* that this game is for the

NBA championship. And' I want you to *pretend* that you're on a three-game winning streak. Now go get 'em!"

So the Hawks played their hearts out that night—and the Boston Celtics handed them their heads in a sack. It was a massacre. Cotton was stunned by the magnitude of the loss. As he stood on the court at the end of the game, staring up at the scoreboard in disbelief, our All-Star guard, Pete Maravich, sauntered past Coach Fitzsimmons and slapped him on the back. "Cheer up, Coach," he said. "Just *pretend* we won!"

Maravich was one of the most exciting basketball showmen of all time, with his behind-the-back dribble, his between-the-legs pass, his pinpoint shots from way downtown. (Unfortunately, however, he played most of his career before the advent of the three-pointer.) Pistol Pete's hotdogging style and playground moves delighted the fans while offending many purists. His fat paycheck annoyed his teammates—he was the first NBA player to land a million-dollar contract. He had ample ego, as demonstrated by the fact that Maravich put his nickname, "Pistol," on the back of his jersey while all other NBA players put only their last name.

Maravich's game was entertaining, and his personal stats were great, but the teams he played on were characterized by mediocre records and poor playoff showings. My year in Atlanta was Pete's final year with the Hawks, and it was his highest-scoring NBA season to date. He averaged 27.7 points per game, second only to the 30.6 posted by Bob McAdoo. Yet our overall record was a dismal 35-47, and we missed the playoffs. Pete worked hard, put on a brilliant show, but he couldn't play within Cotton's system. We didn't have a team—we just had Pete and four other guys who ran up and down the court, watching him shoot.

Basketball Was His Religion

Pete never won a championship, not even at the end of his career, when he played with Larry Bird and the Celtics. In fact, Pete's brief tenure in Boston was one of the few years the Celtics *didn't* win the championship. He retired at the beginning of the 1980-81 season—a decision he later said was due to immaturity and pride. "I didn't need to quit," he reflected. "My last game with the Celtics, I scored 38 points, and that night I quit." The Celtics went on to win the championship that year—without Pistol Pete.

Maravich was embittered after that. He gave or threw away all of his basketball memorabilia and kicked the game out of his life. He lived a hermit's existence, shut up inside his house, and didn't touch a basketball for two years.

Yet he seemed lost without basketball. His mother, Helen, once said that as a boy he had carried a basketball around with him like other kids carry teddy bears. He would go to the matinee, dribbling the ball all the way into the theater. He'd sit on one side of the theater and dribble the ball on the carpet throughout the first movie of a double bill; at

intermission, he'd move to the other side of the theater and dribble with his other hand. The game had been his religion ever since he could remember, and when he gave it up, he killed the only god he'd ever known.

His life began to collapse around him. His mother committed suicide, and Pete blamed himself. His social drinking turned to problem drinking. He was haunted by the question, "Why am I here? Is this all there is to life?" Searching for peace and meaning, he explored drugs, UFOs, astrology, and Eastern mysticism. He contemplated suicide, especially when he was out driving his Porsche down country roads at 140 miles an hour.

"I'll Be With You Soon"

Then, one night in November 1982, while his wife Jackie slept beside him, he lay awake far past midnight. He stared into the darkness as memories flooded his mind—memories of all the hurt he had caused himself and others over the years through his sin and selfishness. As the dark hours passed, the most painful and shameful moments of his life were replayed in his mind. He tried to shut them out, but couldn't.

"Finally," he recalled, "at about 5:40 in the morning, while it was still dark, I cried out in my spirit to a God I didn't know. I said, 'Oh God, can You save me? Can You forgive me?' I didn't know anything about God. My parents had taken me to church and Sunday school, but I didn't remember anything I heard there. I had never read the Bible, and I didn't know if God could ever love someone who

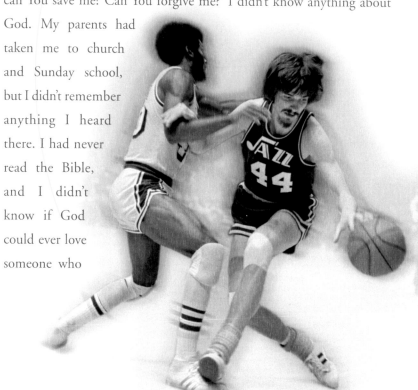

had done all the things I had done. So I said, 'God, if You don't save me, nothing will save me.' Then I remembered a prayer I had heard at camp, seventeen years earlier."

As a nineteen year old, he had gone with a friend to a Christian sports camp. There, he had heard about Jesus Christ. Pete's friend prayed a prayer, committing his life to Christ. But Pete didn't think he needed Jesus, so he chose to go his own way. Almost two decades later, the prayer he had refused as a teenager came back to his mind. "It was a simple prayer," Maravich recalled. "It just said, 'Jesus, I believe You died and rose again. I ask You to come and take over my life.' I didn't know anything about the Bible or theology. All I knew was Jesus."

He got out of bed and shook his wife, waking her. "Jackie!" he said excitedly, "I'm going to be saved! I know it!" But she had seen him go through Eastern religion and other phases, so she said, "That's nice, Pete," and went back to sleep.

But Pete knew this was like nothing that had ever happened to him before. "It was no feeling, just fact," he later recalled. "Jesus had changed me. He had changed my whole life. It wasn't an emotional experience, but I knew it was real. Ever since that morning, I have been assured of my salvation. There's no doubt."

For the next five years, Pete Maravich became a dedicated evangelist for Jesus Christ. He told anyone who would listen that Jesus is the answer to all of life's questions and problems. In 1987, he addressed thirty-five thousand people at a Billy Graham Crusade in Columbia, South Carolina. "Next week I'll be inducted into the Hall of Fame," he said, "but I wouldn't trade my position in Christ for a thousand NBA championships, for a thousand Hall of Fame rings, or for a hundred billion dollars."

After his induction into the Hall of Fame, he reflected, "My whole life I had strived after one thing: The championship ring. I thought it would bring me happiness, but I never caught it. I did get a Hall of Fame ring when I was inducted. When I looked at that ring, the words of Jesus from Matthew 16:26 came to my mind: 'For what profit is it to a man if he gains the whole world, and loses his own soul? Or what will a man give in exchange for his soul?'"

That same year, Pete's father, who was a Christian, lay dying of bone cancer. In the closing moments of his dad's life, Pete leaned over and whispered in his father's ear, "I want you to know, Dad, that I'll be with you soon." Though his medical checkups had always shown him to be in good health, Pete Maravich had a mysterious sense that his own time was short.

Looking Unto Jesus

Pete was invited to appear as a guest on the radio program of the noted Christian psychologist and author, Dr. James Dobson. Dr. Dobson asked Pete to come out early and play a pickup game with him at a gym in Pasadena. After they had played for about 45 minutes, Dr. Dobson said, "Pete, you can't give up this game! You're too good, and you enjoy it too much."

Maravich said, "This is the first time I've played in almost a year. But I haven't really felt well lately. I've had this pain in my chest."

Concerned, Dr. Dobson asked, "How do you feel today?"

"Today I feel great!" said Pistol Pete. Those were his last words.

Dr. Dobson started to walk away to get a drink of water, but he looked back and saw Pete Maravich collapse to the gym floor. Dr. Dobson and another man took turns applying CPR while someone called 911—but Maravich was already gone. An autopsy later revealed a previously undetected heart defect, an unconnected left coronary artery. Few people with that defect live past age thirty; doctors were amazed he had survived a ten-year NBA career. He was forty when he died on January 5, 1988, and he was wearing a tee shirt that read, "Looking Unto Jesus."

True to his word, Pete Maravich joined his father in eternity. Before he left, Pete managed to cram a whole lifetime of service to God into five short years. That's the way I want to live my life—and that's the way I want to leave this world when my time comes: looking unto Jesus. Pete prayed a simple prayer in November 1982, and it changed his entire life. I prayed that same prayer in February 1968, and it transformed my life as well.

How about you? Does your life need to be changed right now? Are you ready to pray that prayer? Then say these words from the depths of your heart: "Jesus, I'm a sinner, and I have no hope but You. I believe You died and rose again. I ask You to come and take over my life."

The change that comes over your life may not be a feeling, but it will be a fact. You've got God's Word on it: ". . . whoever calls on the name of the LORD shall be saved" (Rom. 10:13).

Acknowledgments

I would like to acknowledge the following people for their effort, support, and encouragement during the writing of this book:

Thanks to Jim Denney for his imagination and insight. This is our sixth collaboration—and I think it is one of our best. Thanks, also, to my friends Jack Countryman and Jenny Baumgartner for making this book a work of visual power and basketball splendor.

Special thanks to Bob Vander Weide, president and CEO of RDV Sports, and the entire RDV Sports family; my assistant Melinda Ethington—thank you for your commitment and hard work; my ace typist, Fran Thomas; and to Sam Elmer and Hank Martens of the mailroom and copy room at RDV Sports—your willingness to always help me is appreciated.

A big thank you goes to my proof-readers/fact-checkers/critics: to my longtime friend Ken Hussar; and to Harvey Pollack of the Philadelphia 76ers public relations/publicity staff.

My thanks to Dave Branon of *Sports Spectrum* magazine for time spent researching and providing material for this book. All quotations from *Sports Spectrum* are used by permission. (*Sports Spectrum*, a Christian sports magazine, Grand Rapids, MI. For subscription information, call 1-800-283-8333.)

And thanks to David Smale and Debbie Snow of the Fellowship of

Christian Athletes World Headquarters, 8701 Leeds Road, Kansas City, MO 64129, for time spent researching and providing material for this book. All quotations from the Fellowship of Christian Athletes' *Sharing the Victory* magazine are used by permission. For subscription information, call 1-800-289-0909.

And as always, special thanks to my wife, Ruth, for her patient love and support in everything I do.

Grateful acknowledgments for quotations included in this book are made to the following sources:

Ellis, LaPhonso. "A Whole New Ball Game" by Will Greer, Fellowship of Christian Athletes' *Sharing the Victory*, February 1996, p. 6.

Erving, Julius. "Catching Up With . . . Julius Erving" by Tom Felton, *Sports Spectrum*, March-April 1993, p. 15.

Garnett, Kevin. "The Game Is Still a Joy" by Kelly Whiteside, *Sports Illustrated*, 1 November 1996, p. 36.

Green, A. C. "A. C. Green Lives Like a Champion" by Joel M. Horn, Fellowship of Christian Athletes' *Sharing the Victory*, February 1995, p. 9; "Withstanding the Pressure" by Ken Walker, Fellowship of Christian Athletes' *Sharing the Victory*, February 1993, p. 14; "The A. C. Green Against the Flow" by Kevin Hunter, *Sports Spectrum*, December 1995, pp. 6-8; "Green Never Gives In To Temptations" by Dave George, *The Palm Beach Post*, 13 April 2001, p. 1B.

Hawkins, Hersey. "Standing Tall and Soaring High" by Tom Felton, Fellowship of Christian Athletes' *Sharing the Victory*, January 1997, p. 7.

Johnson, Avery. "The Little Guard That Could" by Rob Bentz, *Sports Spectrum*, November 1993, pp. 15-19; "NBA: Inspurational" by Jeff Ryan, *The Sporting News*, 5 July 1999, pp. 36-40; "The Inner Game: Braking The Break" by Marty Burns, *Sports Illustrated*, 13 April 1998, p. 89; "Spurs Of The Moment" by Phil Taylor, *Sports Illustrated*, 7 July 1999, pp 82ff.; "Avery Johnson: The Little Guard Who Could" by Lars Anderson, *Sports Illustrated*, 7 July 1999, pp. 44ff.

Mutumbo, Dikembe. "Point Man" by Victor Lee, *Sports Spectrum*, March 2000, pp. 25-27.

Price family—Denny, Mark, and Brent. "Family Faith: A Christian Clan from Enid" by Mark Rountree, Fellowship of Christian Athletes' *Sharing the Victory*, November 1992, pp. 8-9; "Straight Talk With Brent Price" (interview), *Sports Spectrum*, March 2000, p. 3; "New Title Suits Price Perfectly" by John D. Pierce, Crosswalk.com Sports, electronically retrieved at http://sports.crosswalk.com/ncaabasketball/articles/item/1,,3597,00.htm; "Mark Price's Father Dies," *The Atlanta Journal and Constitution*, 8 July 2000, p. E11.

Rivers, Doc. "Pressure? What Pressure?" by Charles P. Pierce, *Esquire*, 1 December 2000, pp. 80ff., electronically retrieved at elibrary.com.

Robinson, David. "A New Psalm for David" by Brad Townsend, Fellowship of Christian Athletes' *Sharing the Victory*, January 1992, p. 5; "Robinson for Three" by Rob Bentz, *Sports Spectrum*, June 1996, p. 15; Robinson, David. "Trials of David" by Leigh Montville, *Sports Illustrated*, 29 April 1996, pp. 90ff; "The Hard Truth:

Robinson Isn't Soft" by David DuPree, *USA Today*, 2 June 1999, p. 3C; "Straight Talk With David Robinson," author unavailable, *Sports Spectrum*, electronically retrieved at http://sports.crosswalk.com/spectrum/straighttalk/0,6661,5340,00.htm.

Van Gundy, Jeff. "God in the Locker Room" by John Rowe, *The Bergen Record*, 15 April 2001, p. S1.

Ward, Charlie. "A Humble Champion for Christ" by Robbie Burns, Fellowship of Christian Athletes' *Sharing the Victory*, March 1994, p. 6.

Westphal, Paul. "Westphal Well Worth Wait" by Mark Whicker, *The Arizona Republic*, 29 November 1998, p. C1; "Catching Up With . . . Paul Westphal," author unavailable, *Sports Spectrum*, July-August 1991, p. 29.

Williams, Buck. "The Buck Stops Here" by Steve Matthies, Fellowship of Christian Athletes' *Sharing the Victory*, April 1991, pp. 8-9; "After 17 Seasons, Buck Calls It Quits" by John Jeansonne, *Newsday*, 28 January 1999, p. A95; "Buck Williams Ends Career" by Steve Adamek, *The Bergen Record*, 28 January 1999, p. S8; "A Worthy Buck" by John Brennan, *The Bergen Record*, 11 April 1999, p. S8.

Wood, David. "Childhood Lessons Pay Longterm Dividends in Basketball for David Wood" by Dean Jackson, Fellowship of Christian Athletes' *Sharing the Victory*, April 1998, pp. 21-23.

You can contact Pat Williams directly:

Pat Williams
c/o RDV Sports
8701 Maitland Summit Boulevard
Orlando, FL 32810
(407) 916-2404
pwilliams@rdvsports.com

If you would like to set up a speaking engagement
for Pat Williams, please call or write to his assistant,
Melinda Ethington, at the above address or call
her at (407) 916-2454. Requests can also be
faxed to (407) 916-2986 or e-mailed to
methington@rdvsports.com.